Smart Start
Read & Write

1
Grade 1

This book belongs to

_____

Name

Writing: Barbara Allman
Content Editing: Lisa Vitarisi Mathews
Joy Evans
Copy Editing: Laurie Westrich
Art Direction: Yuki Meyer
Cover Design: Yuki Meyer
Cover Illustration: Chris Lensch
Illustration: Ann Iosa
Design/Production: Jessica Onken

EMC 2429

Helping Children Learn

Visit
teaching-standards.com
to view a correlation
of this book.
This is a free service.

**Correlated to
Current Standards**

**Congratulations on your purchase of some of the
finest teaching materials in the world.**

EVAN-MOOR CORP.
phone 1-800-777-4362, fax 1-800-777-4332.
Entire contents © 2019 EVAN-MOOR CORP.
18 Lower Ragsdale Drive, Monterey, CA 93940-5746. Printed in China.

CPSIA: Asia Pacific Offset Ltd, Kowloon, Hong Kong [6/2019]

Contents

How to Use This Book **4**

Weekly Lessons

Snap, Tap, Clap—**am, ap** **6**

Stan the Cat—**an, at** **12**

Review It!—**am, ap, an, at** **18**

Will a Hen Get Wet?—**en, et** **22**

Nell and the Red Sled—**ell, ed** **28**

Review It!—**en, et, ell, ed** **34**

Can Miss Tig Win?—**ig, in** **38**

Let's Knit—**ip, it** **44**

Review It!—**ig, in, ip, it** **50**

Bob's Shop—**ob, op** **54**

Dog Meets Frog—**og, ot** **60**

Review It!—**ob, op, og, ot** **66**

Fun in a Tub—**ub, ug** **70**

Out Goes the Junk—**um, unk** **76**

Review It!—**ub, ug, um, unk** **82**

Slide, Glide, Ride on Ice—**ice, ide** **86**

Snow Day—**old, ow** **92**

Dune Lake—**ue, une** **98**

At the Beach—**each, ear** **104**

A Skate Party—**ake, ate** **110**

Review It!—**ice, ide, old, ow, ue, une, each, ear, ake, ate** **116**

Answer Key **121**

How to Use This Book

Helping Your Child Excel at Reading and Writing

Word families, also called phonograms, provide new readers with groups of words that have predictable patterns. Each individual word family has the same ending letters and sounds, so they are rhyming words. This makes learning a group of word family words easy. The activities in this book will help your child learn word family spelling patterns, which will increase your child's reading and writing vocabulary. This combination of practice is a great way to immediately increase your child's reading and writing competencies!

Word Family Stories

Each of the 15 word family stories in this book introduces two word families and includes a full-page illustration. Have your child read the title of the story, look at the illustration, and read the word family words in the box. Then, have your child listen to the audio story. Next, have your child read aloud the story to you. Provide support as your child reads the story. Last, discuss the story with your child as he or she colors the picture.

Spell It! Activities

These activities focus on writing word family words and vocabulary comprehension, in addition to identifying word family chunks. The configuration boxes provide structure for your child to write each word. Provide support as needed as your child completes these activities.

Write It! Activities

These activities focus on reading and writing simple sentences that include words from the focus word families. The traceable font models proper letter formation, and the pictures support sentence comprehension. Provide your child with support as needed as he or she completes the activities.

Read It! Activities

These activities focus on reading and reading comprehension skills, in addition to word meaning. At this point in the unit, your child has encountered the focus words several times and should be able to read the sentences fluently.

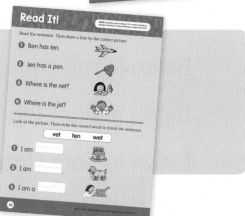

Find It! and Solve It! Activities

The Find It! activities consist of a word search with the unit's focus words. If this type of activity does not support your child's learning style, or your child experiences frustration finding the words, you may wish to skip these activities. The Solve It! activities provide clues for the unit's focus words. Provide your child with support as needed as he or she completes the activities.

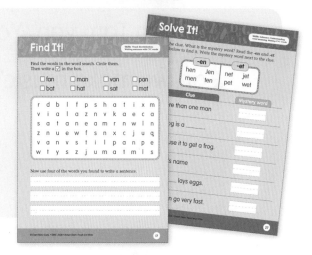

Review It! Activities

These activities provide your child with another opportunity to practice the word families he or she has learned in previous units. The intention is to provide your child with another opportunity to practice the skills and demonstrate mastery.

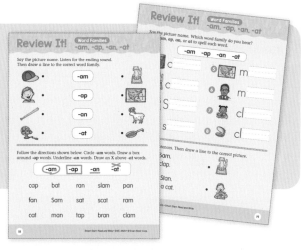

Snap, Tap, Clap

Listen to the story. (Track 2) Then read the story out loud on your own. Listen for words that end with the sounds of **-am** and **-ap**.

Can we make music? Yes, we can!

I can snap. Pam can tap. Sam can clap.

Listen to me snap. Snap, snap, snap.

Listen to Pam tap. Tap, tap, tap.

Listen to Sam clap. Clap, clap, clap.

Oh, I almost forgot Tam! Tam can yap!

Listen to Tam yap. Yap, yap, yap!

Can we make music? Yes, we can!

Smart Start: Read and Write • EMC 2429 • © Evan-Moor Corp.

Read the words. Then color the picture.

-am	-ap
Sam	tap
Pam	yap
Tam	clap

Skills: Reading and writing CVC and CCVC words; Understanding word meaning; Identifying spelling patterns

-am	-ap
ram	map
jam	cap
clam	nap

Look at the picture. Write the correct word in the boxes.

Circle the **-am** words. Underline the **-ap** words.

-am	-ap

nap	dam	Pam	ram	cap	map
jam	tap	clap	snap	Sam	clam

Smart Start: Read and Write • EMC 2429 • © Evan-Moor Corp.

Write It!

Read the sentence. Trace the sentence.
Then write the sentence on the lines below.

1 I am Pam.

2 I can tap.

3 I am Sam.

4 I can clap.

Read It!

Skills: Reading and writing CVC and CCVC words; Reading simple sentences; Demonstrating comprehension

Read the sentence. Then draw a line to the correct picture.

1 I am a clam.

2 I am a ram.

3 I can tap.

4 I can snap.

Look at the picture. Then write the correct word to finish the sentence.

yap	clap	nap

1 I can _____.

2 I can _____.

3 I can _____.

Find the words in the word search. Circle them.
Then write a ✓ in the box.

☐ ram ☐ swam ☐ nap ☐ map
☐ clam ☐ jam ☐ clap ☐ snap

r	d	o	s	r	p	s	w	a	m	i	x	c
v	i	c	l	u	z	i	v	k	a	e	c	l
m	c	l	d	m	e	l	m	a	p	w	l	d
j	n	a	e	w	q	k	c	l	a	p	u	m
a	c	m	s	n	a	p	l	r	n	a	p	i
m	t	y	s	r	a	m	m	x	n	m	l	s

Now use four of the words you found to write a sentence.

Stan the Cat

Stan is my tan cat. Stan likes to sit on the mat. He watches while Mom cooks. One day, he sat on the mat. He was in Mom's way. Mom wanted Stan to move. She had a pan. She said, "Scat, cat! Scat, cat! Scat, cat!" But Stan sat and sat. Mom turned on the cooking fan. That cat ran! I guess Stan did not like the fan. Maybe next time Mom says, "Scat, cat!" Stan will not sit on the mat—he will scat!

Read the words. Then color the picture.

-an	**-at**
fan	cat
pan	hat
man	mat

Spell It!

Skills: Reading and writing CVC words; Understanding word meaning; Identifying spelling patterns

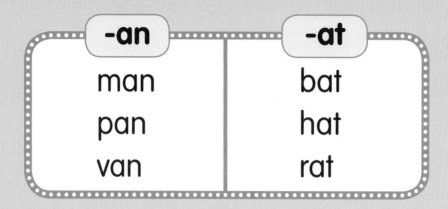

-an	-at
man	bat
pan	hat
van	rat

Look at the picture. Write the correct word in the boxes.

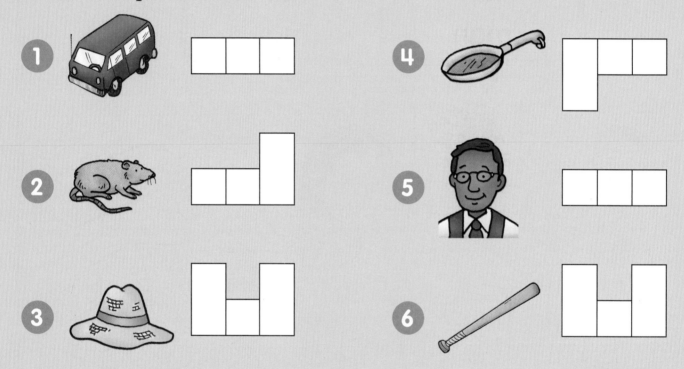

1   **2**   **3**   **4**   **5**   **6**

Circle the **-an** words. Underline the **-at** words.

-an	-at

tan	Stan	pan	rat	van	plan
mat	cat	hat	fan	bat	ran

Smart Start: Read and Write • EMC 2429 • © Evan-Moor Corp.

Write It!

Skills: Reading and writing CVC words; Reading and writing simple sentences

Read the sentence. Trace the sentence.
Then write the sentence on the lines below.

1 The cat sat.

2 It sat on a mat.

3 See the fan.

4 The cat ran.

Read It!

Skills: Reading and writing CVC words; Reading simple sentences; Demonstrating comprehension

Read the sentence. Then draw a line to the correct picture.

1 I can fan.

2 I am tan.

3 That is a bat.

4 That is a rat.

Look at the picture. Then write the correct word to finish the sentence.

bat	hat	man

1 I see the _____.

2 I see the _____.

3 I see the _____.

Find It!

Skills: Visual discrimination;
Writing sentences with CVC words

Find the words in the word search. Circle them.
Then write a ✓ in the box.

☐ fan ☐ man ☐ van ☐ pan

☐ bat ☐ hat ☐ sat ☐ mat

r	d	b	l	f	p	s	h	a	t	i	x	m
v	i	a	l	a	z	n	v	k	a	e	c	a
s	a	t	a	n	e	a	m	r	n	w	l	n
z	n	u	e	w	f	s	n	x	c	j	u	q
v	a	n	v	s	t	i	l	p	a	n	p	e
w	t	y	s	z	j	u	m	a	t	m	l	s

Now use four of the words you found to write a sentence.

_____

_____

_____

Word Families
-am, -ap, -an, -at

Say the picture name. Listen for the ending sound.
Then draw a line to the correct word family.

-am

-ap

-an

-at

Follow the directions shown below. Circle **-am** words. Draw a box around **-ap** words. Underline **-an** words. Draw an **X** above **-at** words.

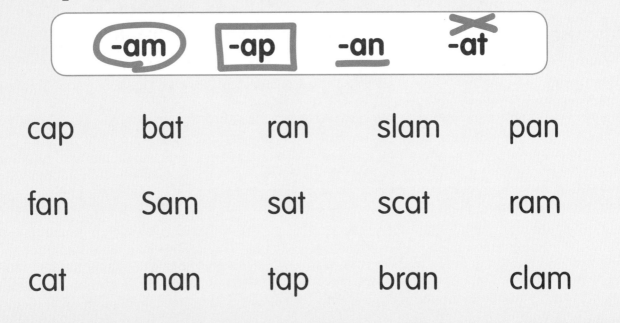

cap	bat	ran	slam	pan
fan	Sam	sat	scat	ram
cat	man	tap	bran	clam

Smart Start: Read and Write • EMC 2429 • © Evan-Moor Corp.

Review It!

Say the picture name. Which word family do you hear?
Write **am**, **ap**, **an**, or **at** to spell each word.

| -am | -ap | -an | -at |

1. c____

2. c____

3. S____

4. s____

5. m____

6. m____

7. cl____

8. cl____

· ·

Read the sentences. Then draw a line to the correct picture.

1. I am Sam.
   I can clap.

2. This is Stan.
   Stan is a cat.

Review It!

Read the words in the box. Look at the picture.
Then write the correct word to finish the sentence.

ram	cat	jam	fan	pan
mat	clap	rat	clam	pan

1 The _____ sat.

2 I see the _____ .

3 That is a _____ .

4 I can _____ .

5 The _____ is big.

Look at the picture. Then write a sentence about it.

_____

Review It!

Look at the picture.
Then use the words in the box to write a sentence on the lines.

tap Pam I it. see

a fan. cat The ran from

Use the words in the box, plus some of your own words,
to write a sentence. Then draw a picture about it.

rat nap

21

Will a Hen Get Wet?

Listen to the story. (Track 4) Then read the story out loud on your own. Listen for words that end with the sounds of **-en** and **-et**.

One day, a hen discovered that the pen gate was open. Soon, ten hens were gone! They went down to the pond. Some ducks were playing in the pond. "Hi, hens. Come in and get wet," quacked the ducks. "We do not like to get wet," clucked the hens. Not like to get wet? Not like to get wet? The ducks were upset. Everyone likes to get wet! "We are not ducks. We are hens," said the hens. "Don't be upset. We don't like to get wet. We better go home to our pen." And just like that, the ten hens ran back into their pen before anyone knew they were gone!

Read the words. Then color the picture.

-en	-et
hen	wet
pen	met
ten	get

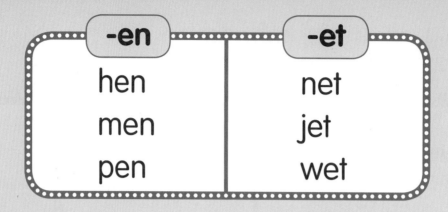

-en	-et
hen	net
men	jet
pen	wet

Look at the picture. Write the correct word in the boxes.

Circle the **-en** words. Underline the **-et** words.

-en	-et

wet   pen   get   hen   set   then

yet   pet   ten   met   vet   let

Write It!

Skills: Reading and writing CVC words; Reading and writing simple sentences

Read the sentence. Trace the sentence.
Then write the sentence on the lines below.

1 See the hen?

2 Are there ten?

3 We met ducks.

4 They get wet.

Read It!

Skills: Reading and writing CVC words; Reading simple sentences; Demonstrating comprehension

Read the sentence. Then draw a line to the correct picture.

1 Ben has ten.

2 Jen has a pen.

3 Where is the net?

4 Where is the jet?

Look at the picture. Then write the correct word to finish the sentence.

| vet | ten | wet |

1 I am _____.

2 I am _____.

3 I am a _____.

Smart Start: Read and Write • EMC 2429 • © Evan-Moor Corp.

Solve It!

Read the clue. What is the mystery word? Read the **-en** and **-et** words below to find it. Write the mystery word next to the clue.

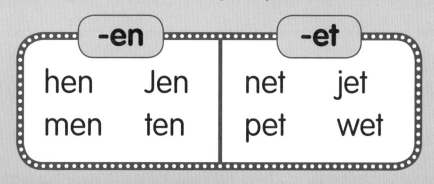

-en		-et	
hen	Jen	net	jet
men	ten	pet	wet

Clue	Mystery word
1 more than one man	
2 A dog is a _____.	
3 You use it to get a frog.	
4 a girl's name	
5 A _____ lays eggs.	
6 This can go very fast.	

Nell and the Red Sled

Listen to the story. (Track 5) Then read the story out loud on your own. Listen for words that end with the sounds of **-ell** and **-ed**.

Last night it snowed. This morning, I got my red sled from the shed. My dog Nell and I went to the park. We pulled the sled to the top of the hill. Then I got on. I gave a yell as I sped on my sled. I sped, and sped, and sped down the hill on my sled. Nell chased me all the way. At the bottom of the hill, I fell into the snow. Nell jumped onto the sled and barked. She wanted to ride on the red sled, too!

Smart Start: Read and Write • EMC 2429 • © Evan-Moor Corp.

Read the words. Then color the picture.

-ell	-ed
fell	red
yell	sled
Nell	sped

Spell It!

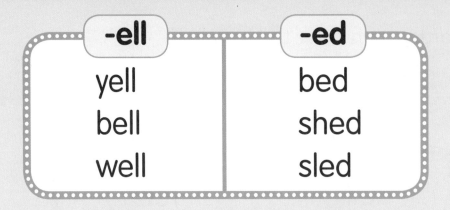

-ell	**-ed**
yell	bed
bell	shed
well	sled

Look at the picture. Write the correct word in the boxes.

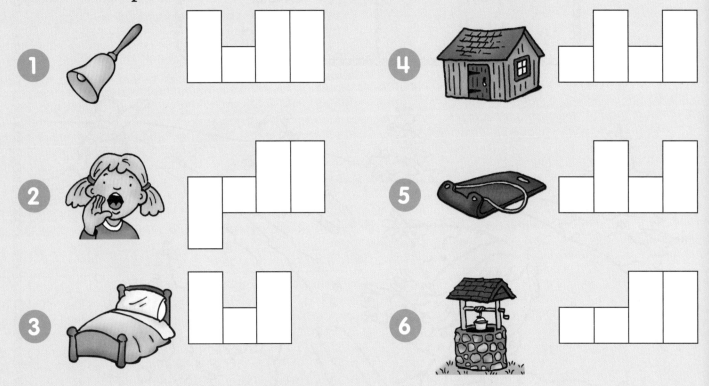

1

2

3

4

5

6

Circle the **-ell** words. Underline the **-ed** words.

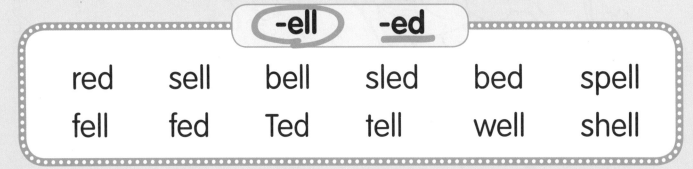

-ell   **-ed**

red	sell	bell	sled	bed	spell
fell	fed	Ted	tell	well	shell

Write It!

Skills: Reading and writing CVC and CCVC words; Reading and writing simple sentences

Read the sentence. Trace the sentence.
Then write the sentence on the lines below.

1 My sled is red.

2 I sped on a sled.

3 I yell to Nell.

4 I tell her I fell.

Read It!

Read the sentence. Then draw a line to the correct picture.

1 The sled is red.

2 Ted is in bed.

3 Hear me yell.

4 I hear the bell.

Look at the picture. Then write the correct word to finish the sentence.

| bell | sled | shell |

1 I have a _____ .

2 I have a _____ .

3 I have a _____ .

Smart Start: Read and Write • EMC 2429 • © Evan-Moor Corp.

Solve It!

Read the clue. What is the mystery word? Read the **-ell** and **-ed** words below to find it. Write the mystery word next to the clue.

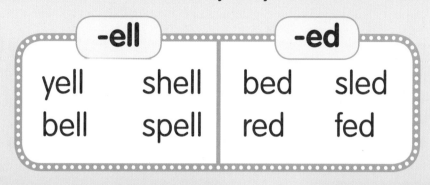

-ell		**-ed**	
yell	shell	bed	sled
bell	spell	red	fed

Clue	Mystery word

1 You sleep in this. _____

2 You learn this at school. _____

3 You find this on a beach. _____

4 This is a color. _____

5 You use this with snow. _____

6 You can _____ outside. _____

Word Families
-en, -et, -ell, -ed

Say the picture name. Listen for the ending sound.
Then draw a line to the correct word family.

-en

-et

-ell

-ed

Follow the directions shown below. Circle **-en** words. Draw a box
around **-et** words. Underline **-ell** words. Draw an **X** above **-ed** words.

red	Nell	jet	get	hen
sell	yet	pen	fed	yell
ten	Ted	vet	spell	let

Review It!

Say the picture name. Which word family do you hear?
Write **en**, **et**, **ell**, or **ed** to spell each word.

| -en | -et | -ell | -ed |

1. b _____
2. b _____
3. sh _____
4. sh _____

5. p _____
6. p _____
7. w _____
8. w _____

Read the sentences. Then draw a line to the correct picture.

1. The duck will get wet.
   The hen will not.

2. I sped on my sled.
   I gave a yell to Nell.

Review It!

Read the words in the box. Look at the picture.
Then write the correct word to finish the sentence.

jet	pen	bell	red	sled
wet	ten	net	hen	well

1 I have a red _____.

2 I hear a _____.

3 Ted is _____.

4 I get _____.

5 Where is the _____?

Look at the picture. Then write a sentence about it.

_____

Word Families
-en, -et, -ell, -ed

Look at the picture.
Then use the words in the box to write a sentence on the lines.

wet? hen get Will the

Nell my sled. sped on

Use the words in the box, plus some of your own words,
to write a sentence. Then draw a picture about it.

hen red

Listen to the story. (Track 6) Then read the story out loud on your own. Listen for words that end with the sounds of **-ig** and **-in**.

Miss Tig wanted to win "best fig" at the fair. Then she could wear a big pin. But her figs were too thin. Only big figs could win. Then Miss Tig had an idea. She went to her fig tree. She pulled on a twig and off came a fig! She pulled twig after twig. Soon she had many figs in her basket. She went home with a grin. Miss Tig made fig jam. It was good! She ate it with everything. She took it to the fair. Did she win best fig? No, but she did win best fig jam! Miss Tig put on her big pin with a grin!

Read the words. Then color the picture.

-ig	-in
big	win
fig	thin
twig	grin

Spell It!

Skills: Reading and writing CVC and CCVC words; Understanding word meaning; Identifying spelling patterns

-ig	-in
big	pin
wig	win
dig	chin

Look at the picture. Write the correct word in the boxes.

Circle the **-ig** words. Underline the **-in** words.

-ig	-in

fig	pin	big	fin	wig	tin
twin	jig	grin	chin	dig	twig

Write It!

Skills: Reading and writing CVC and CCVC words; Reading and writing simple sentences

Read the sentence. Trace the sentence.
Then write the sentence on the lines below.

1 Is this Miss Tig?

2 Is her fig big?

- -

3 Make fig jam.

4 Win a pin.

Read It!

Skills: Reading and writing CVC and CCVC words; Reading simple sentences; Demonstrating comprehension

Read the sentence. Then draw a line to the correct picture.

1 I have a fin.

2 I have a grin.

3 I dig and dig.

4 I jig and jump.

Look at the picture. Then write the correct word to finish the sentence.

wig	swig	fig

1 Try a _____.

2 Take a _____.

3 Try on a _____.

Find It!

Skills: Visual discrimination; Writing sentences with CVC and CCVC words

Find the words in the word search. Circle them.
Then write a ✓ in the box.

☐ wig   ☐ twig   ☐ dig   ☐ big
☐ twin   ☐ fin   ☐ chin   ☐ pin

w	d	o	l	t	p	f	i	n	m	i	x	m
i	i	c	l	w	z	d	i	k	u	e	c	o
g	c	l	a	i	e	i	g	r	c	h	i	n
z	d	a	p	n	m	g	z	n	r	j	u	q
v	c	p	v	s	t	i	l	p	b	i	g	i
t	w	i	g	z	j	u	m	p	i	n	l	s

Now use four of the words you found to write a sentence.

_____

_____

_____

Let's Knit

Listen to the story. (Track 7) Then read the story out loud on your own. Listen for words that end with the sounds of **-ip** and **-it**.

Gabe and the other first-graders are on a field trip. They are learning how yarn used to be made. Then they will learn how to knit. Gabe watches the farmer grip a sheep. Clip, snip! Clip, snip! Clip, snip! The sheep loses its wool. The yarn maker washes the wool. She will dip it in colors and hang it up to dry. Drip, drip. Drip, drip. Next, she will sit at a spinning wheel and spin it into yarn. Spin, spin, spin. Now, Gabe can't wait to knit!

Smart Start: Read and Write • EMC 2429 • © Evan-Moor Corp.

Read the words. Then color the picture.

-ip	-it
dip	kit
trip	sit
clip	knit

Skills: Reading and writing CVC and CCVC words; Understanding word meaning; Identifying spelling patterns

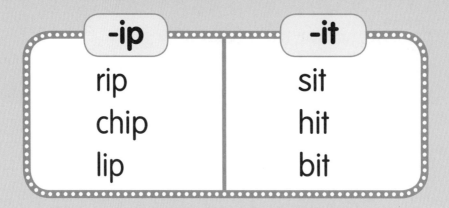

-ip	-it
rip	sit
chip	hit
lip	bit

Look at the picture. Write the correct word in the boxes.

1

2

3

4

5

6

Circle the **-ip** words. Underline the **-it** words.

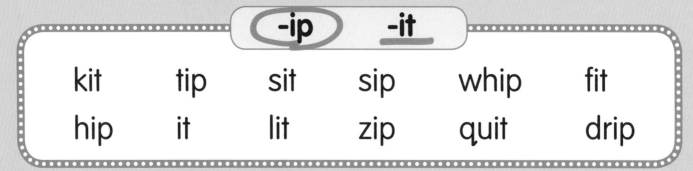

-ip   -it

| kit | tip | sit | sip | whip | fit |
| hip | it | lit | zip | quit | drip |

Write It!

Skills: Reading and writing CVC and CCVC words; Reading and writing simple sentences

Read the sentence. Trace the sentence.
Then write the sentence on the lines below.

1 He will clip it.

2 She will dip it.

---

3 Gabe can knit it.

4 Will it fit?

Read It!

Skills: Reading and writing CVC and CCVC words; Reading simple sentences; Demonstrating comprehension

Read the sentence. Then draw a line to the correct picture.

1 It likes to sit.

2 We like to knit.

3 He took a sip.

4 She took a chip.

Look at the picture. Then write the correct word to finish the sentence.

| sit | trip | ship |

1 Take a _____ .

2 Go on a _____ .

3 You can _____ .

Find It!

Skills: Visual discrimination; Writing sentences with CVC and CCVC words

Find the words in the word search. Circle them.
Then write a ✓ in the box.

☐ sit   ☐ knit   ☐ fit   ☐ quit

☐ ship   ☐ rip   ☐ chip   ☐ lip

r	i	p	l	h	p	s	i	t	d	i	r	m
v	i	c	l	p	z	n	v	k	g	e	c	s
m	c	l	a	s	h	i	p	r	t	l	i	p
z	h	a	e	n	q	u	i	t	r	j	u	q
v	i	p	v	t	i	t	i	k	n	i	t	i
w	p	y	s	z	j	u	m	f	i	t	l	e

Now use four of the words you found to write a sentence.

_____

_____

_____

Review It!

Say the picture name. Listen for the ending sound.
Then draw a line to the correct word family.

-ig

-in

-ip

-it

Follow the directions shown below. Circle **-ig** words. Draw a box around **-in** words. Underline **-ip** words. Draw an **X** above **-it** words.

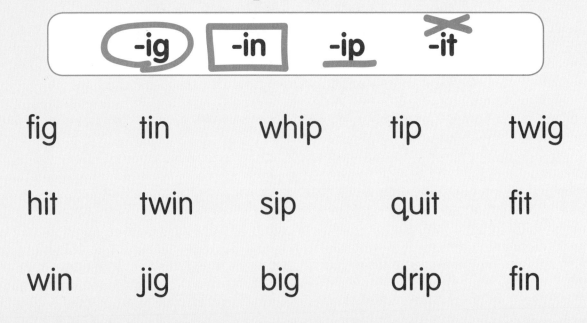

-ig   -in   -ip   -it

fig	tin	whip	tip	twig
hit	twin	sip	quit	fit
win	jig	big	drip	fin

Smart Start: Read and Write • EMC 2429 • © Evan-Moor Corp.

Review It!

Say the picture name. Which word family do you hear?
Write **ig**, **in**, **ip**, or **it** to spell each word.

| -ig | -in | -ip | -it |

1. W _____

2. W _____

3. S _____

4. S _____

5. d _____

6. d _____

7. tw _____

8. tw _____

Read the sentences. Then draw a line to the correct picture.

1. **This fig is thin.**
   Did it win?

2. **I took a chip.**
   I bit it.

Review It!

Read the words in the box. Look at the picture.
Then write the correct word to finish the sentence.

fin	ship	dig	fig	win
knit	grin	chip	sip	twin

1 Would you like a _____?

2 This is how to _____.

3 It has a _____.

4 It is a little _____.

5 It has a _____.

Look at the picture. Then write a sentence about it.

_____

Smart Start: Read and Write • EMC 2429 • © Evan-Moor Corp.

Review It!

Look at the picture.
Then use the words in the box to write a sentence on the lines.

Miss win? Did Tig

went on He a trip.

Use the words in the box, plus some of your own words,
to write a sentence. Then draw a picture about it.

grin big

Bob's Shop

Bob's job is to sell you what you need. He has a shop that is full of handy things. If you need a mop or a knob, go see Bob. If you want something to chop wood, go see Bob. If you need something to pop open a can of paint, go see Bob. Bob knows how to fix most things. He is never too busy to answer questions. If you want to know how to do a job, just ask Bob! If you need something, stop at Bob's shop. You don't have to hop or pop, all you have to do is shop!

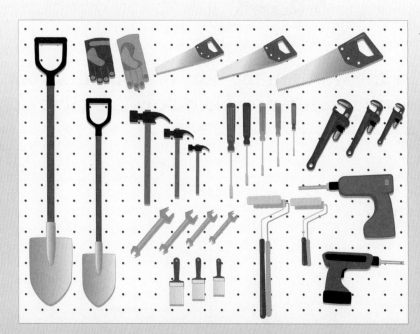

Read the words. Then color the picture.

-ob	-op
Bob	mop
job	shop
knob	stop

Spell It!

Skills: Reading and writing CVC and CCVC words; Understanding word meaning; Identifying spelling patterns

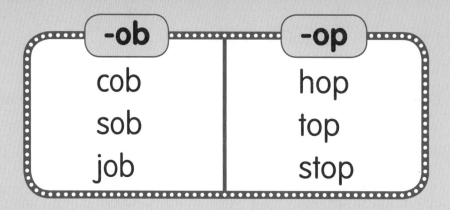

-ob	-op
cob	hop
sob	top
job	stop

Look at the picture. Write the correct word in the boxes.

Circle the **-ob** words. Underline the **-op** words.

-ob	-op
shop Bob top pop mob drop	
mop knob cob rob flop slob	

Smart Start: Read and Write • EMC 2429 • © Evan-Moor Corp.

Read the sentence. Trace the sentence.
Then write the sentence on the lines below.

1 This is Bob's job.

2 He sells a knob.

3 Visit Bob's shop.

4 Buy a mop.

Read It!

Skills: Reading and writing CVC and CCVC words;
Reading simple sentences; Demonstrating comprehension

Read the sentence. Then draw a line to the correct picture.

1 I like it on the cob.

2 I like my job.

3 I like to hop.

4 Did they drop?

Look at the picture. Then write the correct word to finish the sentence.

> **shop   mop   stop**

1 Can you _____?

2 Can you _____?

3 Can you _____?

Smart Start: Read and Write • EMC 2429 • © Evan-Moor Corp.

Solve It!

Read the clue. What is the mystery word? Read the **-ob** and **-op** words below to find it. Write the mystery word next to the clue.

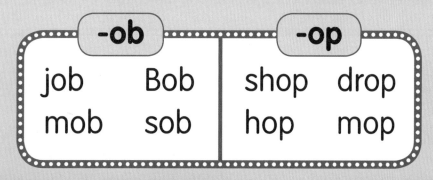

-ob		-op	
job	Bob	shop	drop
mob	sob	hop	mop

Clue	Mystery word
1 a bunny does this	
2 Mom will _____ for food.	
3 You use it to clean.	
4 a boy's name	
5 You work at a _____.	
6 When you cry a lot you _____.	

Dog Meets Frog

Listen to the story. (Track 9) Then read the story out loud on your own. Listen for words that end with the sounds of **-og** and **-ot**.

My dog Dot is friendly. She likes people. She also likes animals. I take her with me when I jog. She likes to trot along and wag her tail. We jog in rain, sun, or fog. Every time we spot an animal, Dot stops. "It's not time to stop yet, Dot," I tell her. "Let's jog." One day, we jogged by a log. On it sat a frog. Dot wagged her tail and sniffed the frog. All of a sudden, the frog said "Croak!" and jumped off its spot on the log. I guess I should have known a frog wouldn't want to be sniffed by a dog. Next time we'll know not to bother a frog on a log.

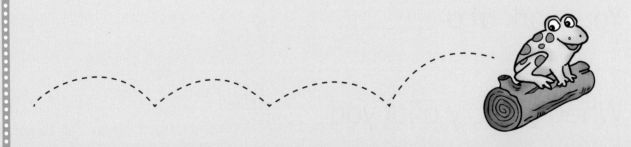

Smart Start: Read and Write • EMC 2429 • © Evan-Moor Corp.

Read the words. Then color the picture.

-og	**-ot**
dog	Dot
jog	spot
fog	trot

Spell It!

Skills: Reading and writing CVC and CCVC words; Understanding word meaning; Identifying spelling patterns

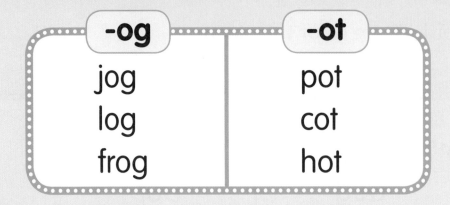

-og	-ot
jog	pot
log	cot
frog	hot

Look at the picture. Write the correct word in the boxes.

Circle the **-og** words. Underline the **-ot** words.

-og	-ot

fog	dot	tot	got	log	jog
spot	dog	not	frog	lot	smog

Smart Start: Read and Write • EMC 2429 • © Evan-Moor Corp.

Write It!

Skills: Reading and writing CVC and CCVC words; Reading and writing simple sentences

Read the sentence. Trace the sentence.
Then write the sentence on the lines below.

1 My dog is Dot.

2 Dot can trot.

3 Frog is on a log.

4 Frog is off a log.

Read It!

Skills: Reading and writing CVC and CCVC words; Reading simple sentences; Demonstrating comprehension

Read the sentence. Then draw a line to the correct picture.

1 I went for a jog.

2 I ran over a log.

3 Is it fog or smog?

4 Is it a dog or a frog?

Look at the picture. Then write the correct word to finish the sentence.

| knot | clog | spot |

1 It has a _____ .

2 It has a _____ .

3 It has a _____ .

Smart Start: Read and Write • EMC 2429 • © Evan-Moor Corp.

Solve It!

Skills: Inference; Understanding word meaning; Writing CVC and CCVC words

Read the clue. What is the mystery word? Read the **-og** and **-ot** words below to find it. Write the mystery word next to the clue.

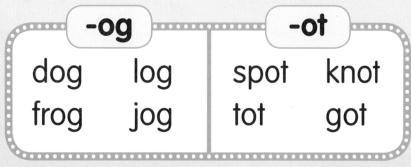

-og		-ot	
dog	log	spot	knot
frog	jog	tot	got

Clue	Mystery word

1 when you run

2 a part of a tree

3 This is a pet.

4 a small child

5 a green animal

6 This is hard to untie.

Say the picture name. Listen for the ending sound.
Then draw a line to the correct word family.

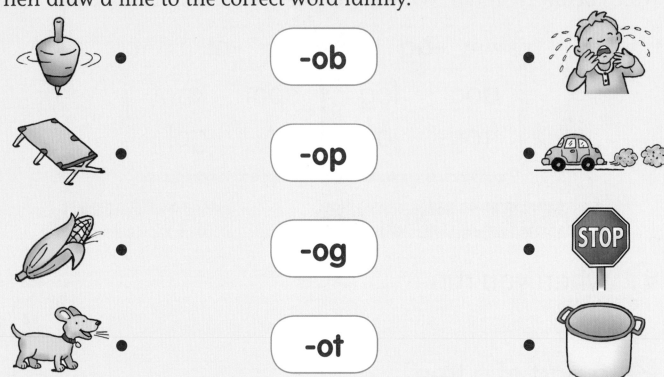

Follow the directions shown below. Circle **-ob** words. Draw a box around **-op** words. Underline **-og** words. Draw an **X** above **-ot** words.

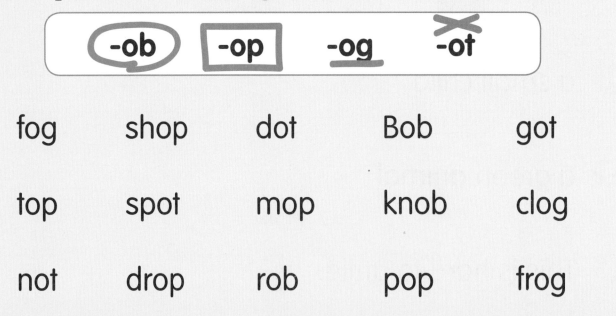

fog	shop	dot	Bob	got
top	spot	mop	knob	clog
not	drop	rob	pop	frog

Review It!

Say the picture name. Which word family do you hear?
Write **ob**, **op**, **og**, or **ot** to spell each word.

| -ob | -op | -og | -ot |

1. d _____
2. d _____
3. c _____
4. c _____
5. j _____
6. j _____
7. kn _____
8. kn _____

Read the sentences. Then draw a line to the correct picture.

1. I have a cob.
   It is hot.

2. That was not a frog.
   That was my dog.

Review It!

Read the words in the box. Look at the picture.
Then write the correct word to finish the sentence.

sob	cot	frog	tot	fog
shop	hot	top	log	hop

1 Here is Bob's _____.

2 Sit on the _____.

3 I am _____.

4 He is a little _____.

5 Why does he _____?

Look at the picture. Then write a sentence about it.

_____

Review It!

Look at the picture.
Then use the words in the box to write a sentence on the lines.

is at shop. the Bob

_____

_____

The is on frog a log.

_____

_____

Use the words in the box, plus some of your own words,
to write a sentence. Then draw a picture about it.

spot dog

_____

_____

Fun in a Tub

Listen to the story. (Track 10) Then read the story out loud on your own. Listen for words that end with the sounds of **-ub** and **-ug**.

Colton loves to take a bath. He fills the tub with warm water and bubbles. He brings his toy sub and sets it on the tub. Then, Colton pretends to be a cub. Next, he pretends his fingers are a water bug. After that, Colton starts to scrub and rub. Scrub, rub, scrub, rub, scrub, rub. When he's done, he tugs on the plug. Tug, tug, tug! He likes to hear the water gurgle down the drain—glug, glug, glug. Colton is a member of the Fun in the Tub Club!

Read the words. Then color the picture.

-ub

cub
tub
club

-ug

bug
tug
plug

Spell It!

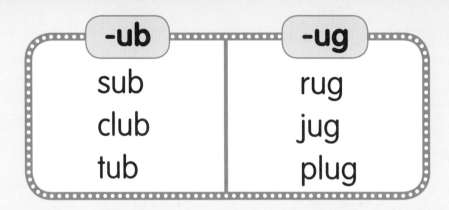

-ub	-ug
sub	rug
club	jug
tub	plug

Look at the picture. Write the correct word in the boxes.

1

2

3

4

5

6

Circle the **-ub** words. Underline the **-ug** words.

-ub	-ug

rub	tug	cub	mug	hug	flub
snug	bug	chug	scrub	hub	stub

Write It!

Skills: Reading and writing CVC and CCVC words; Reading and writing simple sentences

Read the sentence. Trace the sentence.
Then write the sentence on the lines below.

1 I get in the tub.

2 I scrub and rub.

3 Tug on the plug.

4 It goes glug.

Read It!

Skills: Reading and writing CVC and CCVC words; Reading simple sentences; Demonstrating comprehension

Read the sentence. Then draw a line to the correct picture.

1 Where is a slug?

2 Where is a mug?

3 Here is a cub.

4 Here is a shrub.

Look at the picture. Then write the correct word to finish the sentence.

> **bug**   **hug**   **scrub**

1 Can you see a _____ ?

2 Can you _____ ?

3 Can you give a _____ ?

Find It!

Skills: Visual discrimination; Writing sentences with CVC and CCVC words

Find the words in the word search. Circle them.
Then write a ☑ in the box.

☐ tub ☐ scrub ☐ club ☐ rub

☐ bug ☐ hug ☐ slug ☐ plug

r	d	o	l	s	p	l	u	g	r	i	x	m
s	l	u	g	c	z	n	v	k	a	e	c	o
m	c	l	a	r	b	u	g	r	p	r	u	b
z	n	a	e	u	q	h	z	n	r	j	d	q
v	c	p	v	b	t	u	l	u	b	a	p	i
t	u	b	s	z	j	g	m	x	c	l	u	b

Now use four of the words you found to write a sentence.

_____

_____

_____

Out Goes the Junk

Listen to the story. (Track 11) Then read the story out loud on your own. Listen for words that end with the sounds of **-um** and **-unk**.

I knew if Mom saw our room, she would be very glum. We'd flunk her clean-room test! So, my little brother and I made up our bunk beds. Then we put most of our toys into the trunk, all except my brother's toy skunk. I let him keep that on his bed. While we were cleaning, we found some awful junk—a plum pit, a chunk of old wood, gum wrappers, and a broken oatmeal-box drum. Plunk! Into the trash can they went. Now when Mom comes in, we're ready for inspection!

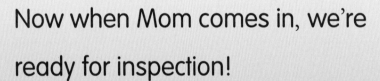

Read the words. Then color the picture.

-um	-unk
gum	bunk
hum	junk
drum	skunk

Spell It!

Skills: Reading and writing CVC and CCVC words; Understanding word meaning; Identifying spelling patterns

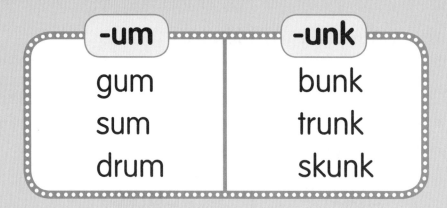

-um	-unk
gum	bunk
sum	trunk
drum	skunk

Look at the picture. Write the correct word in the boxes.

Circle the **-um** words. Underline the **-unk** words.

(-um)	-unk

dunk	hum	mum	junk	plum	hunk
flunk	chum	sunk	strum	plunk	glum

Write It!

Read the sentence. Trace the sentence.
Then write the sentence on the lines below.

1 Toys are in a trunk.

2 Here is my skunk.

3 Do you want gum?

4 Do you want a plum?

Read It!

Skills: Reading and writing CVC and CCVC words; Reading simple sentences; Demonstrating comprehension

Read the sentence. Then draw a line to the correct picture.

1 I can hum.

2 I can strum.

3 I think she can dunk.

4 I think he must have shrunk it.

Look at the picture. Then write the correct word to finish the sentence.

| gum | chunk | plum |

1 I ate a _____.

2 Eat a _____.

3 Have some _____.

Smart Start: Read and Write • EMC 2429 • © Evan-Moor Corp.

Find It!

Skills: Visual discrimination; Writing sentences with CVC and CCVC words

Find the words in the word search. Circle them.
Then write a ✓ in the box.

☐ gum   ☐ plum   ☐ sum   ☐ hum

☐ junk   ☐ sunk   ☐ trunk   ☐ skunk

```
p  l  u  m  h  g  u  m  a  m  t  x  m
v  u  c  l  j  u  n  k  s  a  r  c  k
s  k  u  n  k  e  a  m  u  k  u  l  m
z  n  a  e  w  q  p  t  n  m  n  u  q
v  c  p  v  s  u  m  l  k  j  k  p  i
h  u  m  s  z  j  u  m  x  n  m  l  s
```

Now use four of the words you found to write a sentence.

_____

_____

_____

Say the picture name. Listen for the ending sound.
Then draw a line to the correct word family.

-ub

-ug

-um

-unk

Follow the directions shown below. Circle **-ub** words.
Draw a box around **-ug** words. Underline **-um** words.
Draw an **X** above **-unk** words.

(-ub)   [-ug]   -u̲m̲   -u̶nk

mug	plum	flunk	hug	cub
glum	hum	scrub	trunk	plug
dunk	sub	rub	snug	sunk

Smart Start: Read and Write • EMC 2429 • © Evan-Moor Corp.

Say the picture name. Which word family do you hear?
Write **ub**, **ug**, **um**, or **unk** to spell each word.

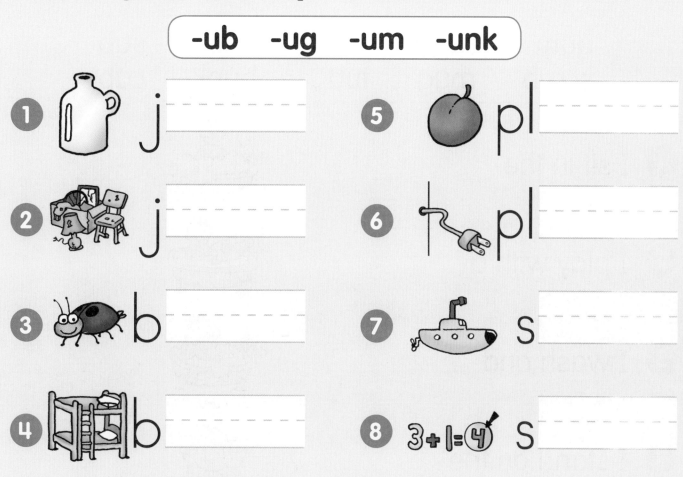

-ub   -ug   -um   -unk

1. j _____

2. j _____

3. b _____

4. b _____

5. pl _____

6. pl _____

7. s _____

8. s _____

- -

Read the sentences. Then draw a line to the correct picture.

1. I have a toy skunk.
   You have gum and a plum.

2. I have a little cub.
   I give my cub a hug.

Review It!

Read the words in the box. Look at the picture.
Then write the correct word to finish the sentence.

hum	rug	dunk	hug	sub
scrub	mug	tub	bunk	cub

1 I sit in the _____ .

2 I play with a _____ .

3 I wash and _____ .

4 I stand on the _____ .

5 I climb into my _____ .

Look at the picture. Then write a sentence about it.

_____

Review It!

Look at the picture.
Then use the words in the box to write a sentence on the lines.

| the I tub. in scrub |

| is on A skunk rug. the |

Use the words in the box, plus some of your own words,
to write a sentence. Then draw a picture about it.

| bug drum |

Slide, Glide, Ride on Ice

Listen to the story. (Track 12) Then read the story out loud on your own. Listen for words that end with the sounds of -**ice** and -**ide**.

It was a wintry night. Snow was on every side. A family of mice had a nice, warm place to hide. They ate their rice and went to sleep. Except for Mo. His eyes were wide open. Mo tiptoed outside to play on the ice. First, he would slide. Then, he would glide. Slide, glide, slide, glide! Next, he took a sled ride! When he went back inside, nobody knew he'd been gone. Mo had been as quiet as a mouse.

Smart Start: Read and Write • EMC 2429 • © Evan-Moor Corp.

Read the words. Then color the picture.

-ice	**-ide**
mice	ride
rice	hide
ice	slide

Spell It!

Skills: Reading and writing CVC and CCVC words; Understanding word meaning; Identifying spelling patterns

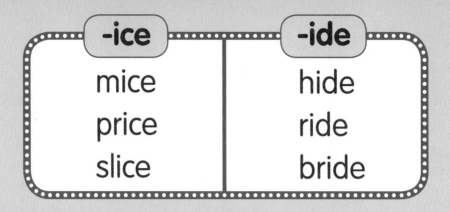

-ice	-ide
mice	hide
price	ride
slice	bride

Look at the picture. Write the correct word in the boxes.

Circle the **-ice** words. Underline the **-ide** words.

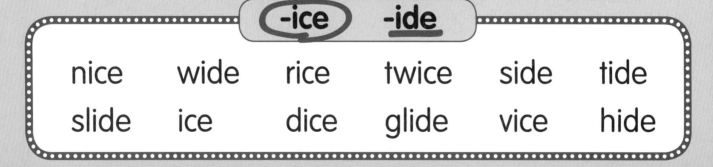

-ice   -ide

nice	wide	rice	twice	side	tide
slide	ice	dice	glide	vice	hide

Write It!

Skills: Reading and writing CVC and CCVC words; Reading and writing simple sentences

Read the sentence. Trace the sentence.
Then write the sentence on the lines below.

1 We are nice mice.

2 We eat rice.

3 I ride and ride.

4 I slide and glide.

Read It!

Skills: Reading and writing CVC and CCVC words; Reading simple sentences; Demonstrating comprehension

Read the sentence. Then draw a line to the correct picture.

1 Where did it hide?

2 Can you slide on it?

3 Do you want a slice?

4 Do you want the dice?

Look at the picture. Then write the correct word to finish the sentence.

bride	price	rice

1 Here is the _____.

2 Here is the _____.

3 Here is the _____.

Smart Start: Read and Write • EMC 2429 • © Evan-Moor Corp.

Solve It!

Read the clue. What is the mystery word? Read the **-ice** and **-ide** words below to find it. Write the mystery word next to the clue.

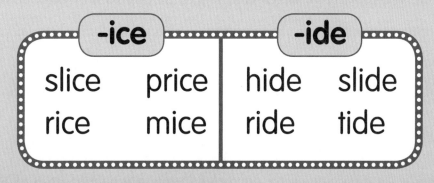

-ice		-ide	
slice	price	hide	slide
rice	mice	ride	tide

Clue	Mystery word

1 You _____ a bike.

2 a _____ of bread

3 how much you pay

4 small animals with tails

5 You go down fast on this.

6 These are small and white.

Snow Day

Listen to the story. (Track 13) Then read the story out loud on your own. Listen for words that end with the sounds of **-old** and **-ow**.

Last night, I heard the cold wind blow. This morning, there's snow! Maybe my school will declare it a snow day, and I can stay home. Dad says it's time for me to get ready for school. "Is it a snow day?" I ask. Dad says it's not. I quickly get dressed and eat so Dad does not scold me for being late. I go outside into the cold and see Dad under the hood of the car. "It won't start," he says. "I had to call for a tow. It could take hours. Looks like it's a snow day for you after all," he smiles.

Smart Start: Read and Write • EMC 2429 • © Evan-Moor Corp.

Read the words. Then color the picture.

-old	**-ow**
cold	tow
hold	snow
scold	know

Spell It!

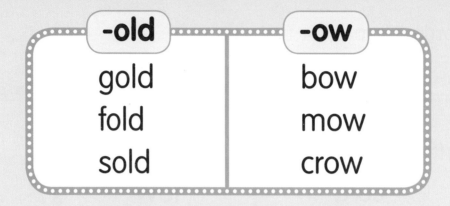

-old	**-ow**
gold	bow
fold	mow
sold	crow

Look at the picture. Write the correct word in the boxes.

Circle the **-old** words. Underline the **-ow** words.

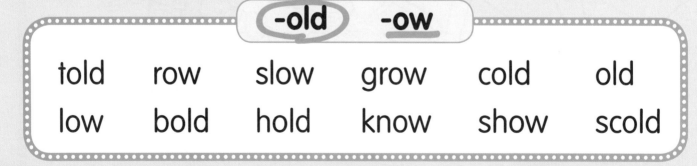

-old	**-ow**

told	row	slow	grow	cold	old
low	bold	hold	know	show	scold

Write It!

Skills: Reading and writing CVC and CCVC words; Reading and writing simple sentences

Read the sentence. Trace the sentence.
Then write the sentence on the lines below.

1 This is cold.

2 It is cold to hold.

3 Look at the snow.

4 Call for a tow.

Read It!

Skills: Reading and writing CVC and CCVC words; Reading simple sentences; Demonstrating comprehension

Read the sentence. Then draw a line to the correct picture.

1 Yours are old.

2 His is gold.

3 Hers is cold.

4 Min's has a bow.

Look at the picture. Then write the correct word to finish the sentence.

scold	hold	show

1 I will _____ him.

2 I will _____ him.

3 I will _____ him.

Solve It!

Skills: Inference; Understanding word meaning; Writing CVC and CCVC words

Read the clue. What is the mystery word? Read the **-old** and **-ow** words below to find it. Write the mystery word next to the clue.

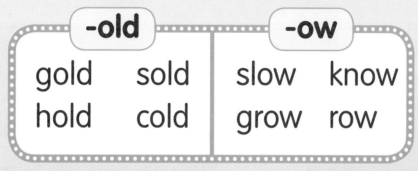

-old		**-ow**	
gold	sold	slow	know
hold	cold	grow	row

Clue	**Mystery word**

1 I am not warm, I am _____.

2 _____ on!

3 It is not fast, it is _____.

4 This is a color.

5 We _____ the car.

6 Do you _____ him?

Dune Lake

It's the month of June, and Sue and her family are going to stay in a cabin at Dune Lake. Sue checks out library books to bring along. They won't be due for three weeks, so she can keep them the whole time she's at the cabin. Sue likes to read nonfiction, or things that are true. She hums a happy tune as she thinks about lying under the sun and reading a book beside the blue water of Dune Lake.

Smart Start: Read and Write • EMC 2429 • © Evan-Moor Corp.

Read the words. Then color the picture.

-ue	-une
blue	June
due	tune
true	dune

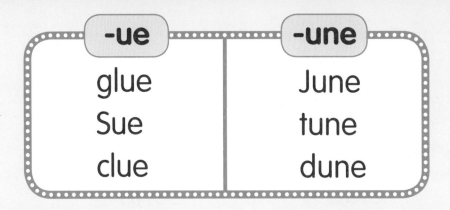

-ue	**-une**
glue	June
Sue	tune
clue	dune

Look at the picture. Write the correct word in the boxes.

1

2

3

4

5

6

Circle the **-ue** words. Underline the **-une** words.

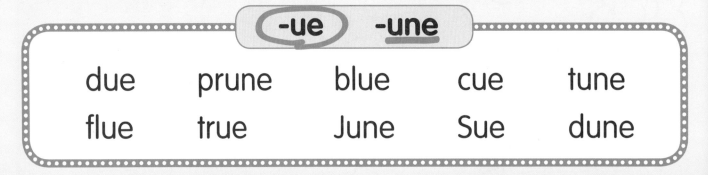

-ue	**-une**

due   prune   blue   cue   tune

flue   true   June   Sue   dune

Write It!

Read the sentence. Trace the sentence.
Then write the sentence on the lines below.

1 I am happy in June.

2 I hum a tune.

3 Sue reads a book.

4 The book is true.

Skills: Reading and writing CVC and CCVC words;
Reading simple sentences; Demonstrating comprehension

Read the sentence. Then draw a line to the correct picture.

1 I have some glue.

2 I have a prune.

3 The sky is blue.

4 The book is true.

Look at the picture. Then write the correct word to finish the sentence.

blue	dune	June

1 We will climb the _____.

2 We like the _____ lake.

3 We will go in _____.

Smart Start: Read and Write • EMC 2429 • © Evan-Moor Corp.

Find It!

Find the words in the word search. Circle them.
Then write a ✓ in the box.

☐ blue   ☐ true   ☐ due   ☐ clue

☐ tune   ☐ june   ☐ dune   ☐ prune

r	t	o	l	b	p	s	w	a	s	i	x	m
v	r	c	d	l	z	n	j	u	n	e	c	d
m	u	r	u	u	p	r	u	n	e	w	l	u
z	e	a	e	e	q	p	z	t	k	j	u	n
v	c	p	v	s	t	u	n	e	n	a	p	e
c	l	u	e	z	j	u	m	x	n	t	l	s

Now use four of the words you found to write a sentence.

_____

_____

_____

At the Beach

Listen to the story. (Track 15) Then read the story out loud on your own. Listen for words that end with the sounds of -**each** and -**ear**.

I go to my dad's every year during summer break. He lives near the beach and teaches me water sports. This year, he is teaching me how to surf. At first, I had a fear of the big waves, but that went away fast. Now I jump onto the surfboard and ride the waves clear to the shore. Every time I hear them hit the sand, I think about surfing. I can't wait until next year—Dad's going to teach me how to water-ski!

Smart Start: Read and Write • EMC 2429 • © Evan-Moor Corp.

Read the words. Then color the picture.

-each	**-ear**
beach	year
teach	fear
reach	hear

Spell It!

Skills: Reading and writing CVC and CCVC words; Understanding word meaning; Identifying spelling patterns

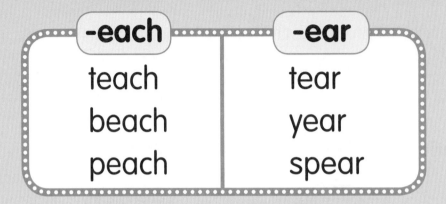

-each	-ear
teach	tear
beach	year
peach	spear

Look at the picture. Write the correct word in the boxes.

Circle the -**each** words. Underline the -**ear** words.

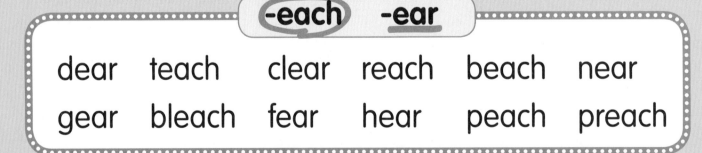

-each   -ear

dear	teach	clear	reach	beach	near
gear	bleach	fear	hear	peach	preach

Write It!

Skills: Reading and writing CVC and CCVC words; Reading and writing simple sentences

Read the sentence. Trace the sentence.
Then write the sentence on the lines below.

1 The beach is near.

2 I can hear it.

3 Here is the beach.

4 Dad will teach me.

Read It!

Skills: Reading and writing CVC and CCVC words; Reading simple sentences; Demonstrating comprehension

Read the sentence. Then draw a line to the correct picture.

1 Which one is near?

2 Which one is clear?

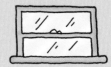

3 I know how to reach it.

4 I know how to teach it.

Look at the picture. Then write the correct word to finish the sentence.

> reach   hear   year

1 I _____ the baby.

2 He can't _____ it.

3 She is one _____ old.

Smart Start: Read and Write • EMC 2429 • © Evan-Moor Corp.

Find It!

Skills: Visual discrimination; Writing sentences with CVC and CCVC words

Find the words in the word search. Circle them.
Then write a ✓ in the box.

☐ teach ☐ reach ☐ beach ☐ peach
☐ hear ☐ fear ☐ dear ☐ near

f	d	e	p	r	p	s	w	a	m	i	x	n
e	t	c	e	a	z	n	d	e	a	r	c	e
a	e	l	a	r	e	a	c	h	p	w	l	a
r	a	a	c	w	q	p	h	e	a	r	u	r
v	c	p	h	s	t	i	l	p	n	a	p	i
w	h	y	s	z	j	u	b	e	a	c	h	s

Now use four of the words you found to write a sentence.

_____

_____

_____

A Skate Party

Listen to the story. (Track 16) Then read the story out loud on your own. Listen for words that end with the sounds of **-ake** and **-ate**.

My friend Jake is having a birthday party on Friday. He can take three friends to Skate World. He invited me to come. Jake's mom is going to bake a cake. She will pick us up at the gate after school. We can skate and play roller tag. After that, we'll each have a plate of cake and ice cream. I'll remember to say, "Thanks for a great party, Jake!"

Smart Start: Read and Write • EMC 2429 • © Evan-Moor Corp.

Read the words. Then color the picture.

-ake
cake
Jake
bake

-ate
gate
skate
plate

Skills: Reading and writing CVC and CCVC words; Understanding word meaning; Identifying spelling patterns

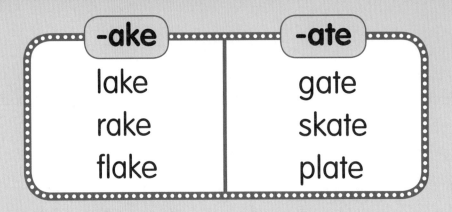

-ake	-ate
lake	gate
rake	skate
flake	plate

Look at the picture. Write the correct word in the boxes.

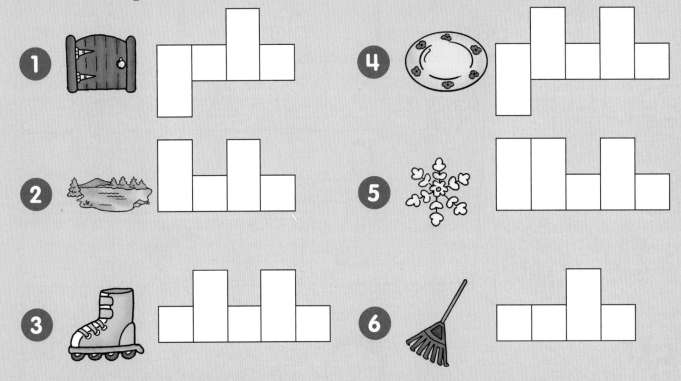

Circle the **-ake** words. Underline the **-ate** words.

-ake	-ate

late	bake	make	date	rate	fake
cake	state	shake	mate	quake	Kate

Write It!

Read the sentence. Trace the sentence.
Then write the sentence on the lines below.

1 Bake a cake.

2 It is for Jake.

3 There is Kate.

4 She can skate.

Read It!

Read the sentence. Then draw a line to the correct picture.

1 Please take this rake.

2 Please take this snake.

3 What is the date?

4 This is a skate.

Look at the picture. Then write the correct word to finish the sentence.

| plate | cake | bake |

1 We like _____.

2 She likes to _____.

3 Put them on a _____.

Solve It!

Skills: Inference; Understanding word meaning; Writing CVC and CCVC words

Read the clue. What is the mystery word? Read the **-ake** and **-ate** words below to find it. Write the mystery word next to the clue.

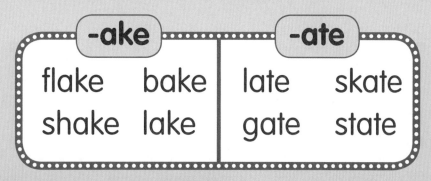

-ake

| flake | bake |
| shake | lake |

-ate

| late | skate |
| gate | state |

Clue	Mystery word
1 a large body of water	____
2 Dad will _____ a cake.	____
3 not on time	____
4 a shoe with wheels	____
5 Close the _____.	____
6 to move up and down	____

Review It!

Say the picture name. Listen for the ending sound.
Then draw a line to the correct word family.

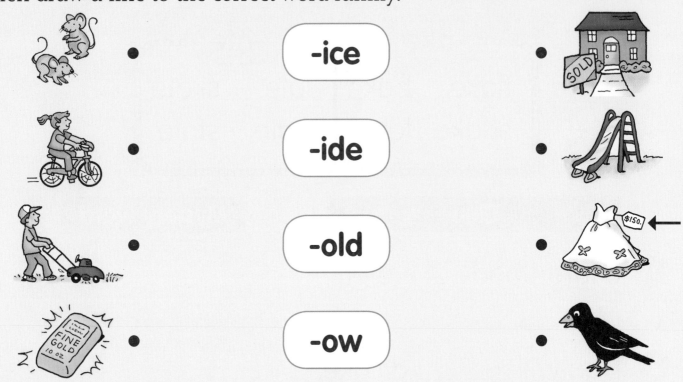

-ice

-ide

-old

-ow

Follow the directions shown below. Circle **-ice** words. Draw a box around
-ide words. Underline **-old** words. Draw an **X** above **-ow** words.

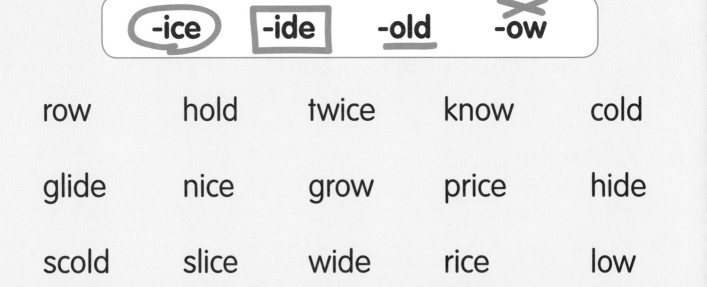

| (-ice) | [-ide] | -old | X̄ -ow |

row	hold	twice	know	cold
glide	nice	grow	price	hide
scold	slice	wide	rice	low

Smart Start: Read and Write • EMC 2429 • © Evan-Moor Corp.

Review It!

Say the picture name. Which word family do you hear?
Write **ue**, **une**, **each**, or **ear** to spell each word.

-ue   -une   -each   -ear

1. t _____

2. p _____

3. J _____

4. t _____

5. sp _____

6. t _____

7. gl _____

8. cl _____

. . . .

Read the sentences. Then draw a line to the correct picture.

1. I am happy in June.
   I hum a tune.

2. The beach is near.
   I can hear it.

Review It!

Read the words in the box. Look at the picture.
Then write the correct word to finish the sentence.

bake	cake	snake	plate	gate
skate	flake	rake	date	lake

1 She will _____ .

2 I see the _____ .

3 That is a _____ .

4 Shut the _____ .

5 The _____ is big.

Look at the picture. Then write a sentence about it.

_____

Smart Start: Read and Write • EMC 2429 • © Evan-Moor Corp.

Look at the picture.
Then use the words in the box to write a sentence on the lines.

a beach. There is at clue the

_____

_____

is plate. rice This on a

_____

_____

Use the words in the box, plus some of your own words,
to write a sentence. Then draw a picture about it.

gate   blue

_____

_____

Answer Key

Page 8

Spell It!
Skills: Reading and writing CVC and CCVC words; Understanding word meaning; Identifying spelling patterns

-am	-ap
ram	map
jam	cap
clam	nap

Look at the picture. Write the correct word in the boxes.

1. j a m
2. m a p
3. c l a m
4. r a m
5. c a p
6. n a p

Circle the **-am** words. Underline the **-ap** words.

-am	-ap

(nap) (dam) (Pam) (ram) <u>cap</u> <u>map</u>
(jam) <u>tap</u> <u>clap</u> <u>snap</u> (Sam) <u>clam</u>

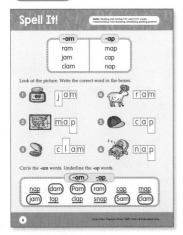

Page 9

Write It!
Skills: Reading and writing CVC and CCVC words; Reading and writing simple sentences

Read the sentence. Trace the sentence.
Then write the sentence on the lines below.

1. I am Pam.
   I am Pam.
2. I can tap.
   I can tap.
3. I am Sam.
   I am Sam.
4. I can clap.
   I can clap.

Page 10

Read It!
Skills: Reading and writing CVC and CCVC words; Reading and writing simple sentences; Demonstrating comprehension

Read the sentence. Then draw a line to the correct picture.

1. I am a clam.
2. I am a ram.
3. I can tap.
4. I can snap.

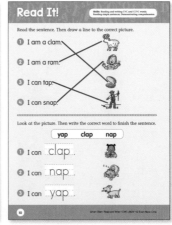

Look at the picture. Then write the correct word to finish the sentence.

yap	clap	nap

1. I can clap.
2. I can nap.
3. I can yap.

Page 11

Find It!
Skills: Visual discrimination; Writing sentences with CVC and CCVC words

Find the words in the word search. Circle them.
Then write a ☑ in the box.

☑ ram ☑ swam ☑ nap ☑ map
☑ clam ☑ jam ☑ clap ☑ snap

```
r d o s r p s w a m i x c
v i c l u z i v k a e c l
m c l d m e l m a p w l d
j n a e w q k c l a p u m
j a c m s n a p l r n a p i
m t y s r a m m x n m l s
```

Now use four of the words you found to write a sentence.

Answers will vary.

Page 14

Spell It!
Skills: Reading and writing CVC words; Understanding word meaning; Identifying spelling patterns

-an	-at
man	bat
pan	hat
van	rat

Look at the picture. Write the correct word in the boxes.

1. v a n
2. r a t
3. h a t
4. p a n
5. m a n
6. b a t

Circle the **-an** words. Underline the **-at** words.

-an	-at

(tan) (Stan) (pan) <u>rat</u> (van) (plan)
<u>mat</u> <u>cat</u> <u>hat</u> (fan) <u>bat</u> (ran)

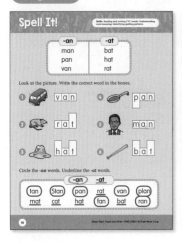

Page 15

Write It!
Skills: Reading and writing CVC words; Reading and writing simple sentences

Read the sentence. Trace the sentence.
Then write the sentence on the lines below.

1. The cat sat.
   The cat sat.
2. It sat on a mat.
   It sat on a mat.
3. See the fan.
   See the fan.
4. The cat ran.
   The cat ran.

Page 16

Read It!
Skills: Reading and writing CVC words; Reading and writing simple sentences; Demonstrating comprehension

Read the sentence. Then draw a line to the correct picture.

1. I can fan.
2. I am tan.
3. That is a bat.
4. That is a rat.

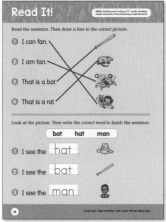

Look at the picture. Then write the correct word to finish the sentence.

bat	hat	man

1. I see the hat.
2. I see the bat.
3. I see the man.

Page 17

Find It!
Skills: Visual discrimination; Writing sentences with CVC words

Find the words in the word search. Circle them.
Then write a ☑ in the box.

☑ fan ☑ man ☑ van ☑ pan
☑ bat ☑ hat ☑ sat ☑ mat

```
r d b l f p s h a t i x m
v i a l a z n v k a e c a
s a t a n e a m r n w l n
z n u e w f s n x c j u q
v a n v s t i l p a n p e
w t y s z j u m a t m l s
```

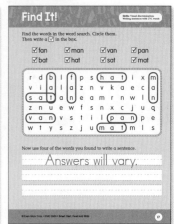

Now use four of the words you found to write a sentence.

Answers will vary.

Page 18

Review It! **Word Families**
-am, -ap, -an, -at

Say the picture name. Listen for the ending sound.
Then draw a line to the correct word family.

-am
-ap
-an
-at

Follow the directions shown below. Circle **-am** words. Draw a box around **-ap** words. Underline **-an** words. Draw an **X** above **-at** words.

-am	-ap	-an	X -at

cap | b̶a̶t̶ | ran | slam | pan
fan | Sam | s̶a̶t̶ | s̶c̶a̶t̶ | ram
c̶a̶t̶ | man | tap | bran | clam

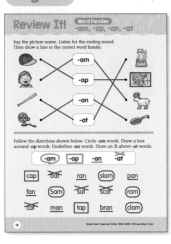

Page 19

Review It! **Word Families**
-am, -ap, -an, -at

Say the picture name. Which word family do you hear?
Write **am**, **ap**, **an**, or **at** to spell each word.

-am	-ap	-an	-at

1. c a n
2. c a t
3. S a m
4. s a t
5. m a p
6. m a n
7. c l a p
8. c l a m

Read the sentences. Then draw a line to the correct picture.

1. I am Sam.
   I can clap.
2. This is Stan.
   Stan is a cat.

Page 20

Review It! **Word Families**
-am, -ap, -an, -at

Read the words in the box. Look at the picture.
Then write the correct word to finish the sentence.

ram	cat	jam	fan	pan
mat	clap	rat	clam	map

1. The cat sat.
2. I see the map.
3. That is a ram.
4. I can clap.
5. The rat is big.

Look at the picture. Then write a sentence about it.

Answers will vary.

Page 21

Review It! **Word Families**
-am, -ap, -an, -at

Look at the picture.
Then use the words in the box to write a sentence on the lines.

tap Pam I it see

I see Pam tap it.

a fan. cat The ran from

The cat ran
from a fan.

Use the words in the box, plus some of your own words, to write a sentence. Then draw a picture about it.

rat nap

Answers will vary.

Page 24

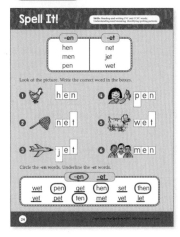

Spell It!
Skills: Reading and writing CVC and CCVC words. Understanding word meaning. Identifying spelling patterns

-en	-et
hen	net
men	jet
pen	wet

Look at the picture. Write the correct word in the boxes.

1. h e n
2. n e t
3. j e t
4. p e n
5. w e t
6. m e n

Circle the **-en** words. Underline the **-et** words.

	-en		-et		
wet	(pen)	get	(hen)	set	(then)
yet	pet	(ten)	met	vet	let

Page 25

Write It!
Skills: Reading and writing CVC words. Reading and writing simple sentences

Read the sentence. Trace the sentence.
Then write the sentence on the lines below.

1. See the hen?
   See the hen?

2. Are there ten?
   Are there ten?

3. We met ducks.
   We met ducks.

4. They get wet.
   They get wet.

Page 26

Read It!
Skills: Reading and writing CVC words. Reading simple sentences. Demonstrating comprehension

Read the sentence. Then draw a line to the correct picture.

1. Ben has ten.
2. Jen has a pen.
3. Where is the net?
4. Where is the jet?

Look at the picture. Then write the correct word to finish the sentence.

vet	ten	wet

1. I am ten.
2. I am wet.
3. I am a vet.

Page 27

Solve It!
Skills: Inference. Understanding word meaning. Writing CVC words

Read the clue. What is the mystery word? Read the **-en** and **-et** words below to find it. Write the mystery word next to the clue.

-en		-et	
hen	Jen	net	jet
men	ten	pet	wet

Clue	Mystery word
1. more than one man	men
2. A dog is a _____	pet
3. You use it to get a frog.	net
4. a girl's name	Jen
5. A _____ lays eggs.	hen
6. This can go very fast.	jet

Page 30

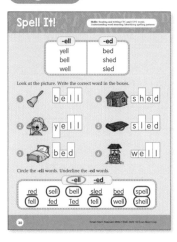

Spell It!
Skills: Reading and writing CVC and CCVC words. Understanding word meaning. Identifying spelling patterns

-ell	-ed
yell	bed
bell	shed
well	sled

Look at the picture. Write the correct word in the boxes.

1. b e l l
2. y e l l
3. b e d
4. s h e d
5. s l e d
6. w e l l

Circle the **-ell** words. Underline the **-ed** words.

	-ell		-ed		
red	(sell)	(bell)	sled	bed	(spell)
(fell)	fed	Ted	(tell)	well	shell

Page 31

Write It!
Skills: Reading and writing CVC and CCVC words. Reading and writing simple sentences

Read the sentence. Trace the sentence.
Then write the sentence on the lines below.

1. My sled is red.
   My sled is red.

2. I sped on a sled.
   I sped on a sled.

3. I yell to Nell.
   I yell to Nell.

4. I tell her I fell.
   I tell her I fell.

Page 32

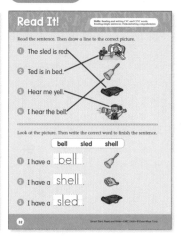

Read It!
Skills: Reading and writing CVC and CCVC words. Reading simple sentences. Demonstrating comprehension

Read the sentence. Then draw a line to the correct picture.

1. The sled is red.
2. Ted is in bed.
3. Hear me yell.
4. I hear the bell.

Look at the picture. Then write the correct word to finish the sentence.

bell	sled	shell

1. I have a bell.
2. I have a shell.
3. I have a sled.

Page 33

Solve It!
Skills: Inference. Understanding word meaning. Writing CVC and CCVC words

Read the clue. What is the mystery word? Read the **-ell** and **-ed** words below to find it. Write the mystery word next to the clue.

-ell		-ed	
yell	shell	bed	sled
bell	spell	red	fed

Clue	Mystery word
1. You sleep in this.	bed
2. You learn this at school.	spell
3. You find this on a beach.	shell
4. This is a color.	red
5. You use this with snow.	sled
6. You can _____ outside.	yell

Page 34

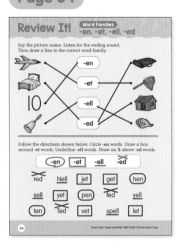

Review It! Word Families
-en, -et, -ell, -ed

Say the picture name. Listen for the ending sound.
Then draw a line to the correct word family.

- -en
- -et
- -ell
- -ed

Follow the directions shown below. Circle **-en** words. Draw a box around **-et** words. Underline **-ell** words. Draw an X above **-ed** words.

-en	-et	-ell	-ed

red Nell jet get hen
sell yet pen yell
ten Ted vet spell let

Page 35

Review It! Word Families
-en, -et, -ell, -ed

Say the picture name. Which word family do you hear?
Write en, et, ell, or ed to spell each word.

-en	-et	-ell	-ed

1. bed
2. bell
3. shed
4. shell
5. pen
6. pet
7. wet
8. well

Read the sentences. Then draw a line to the correct picture.

1. The duck will get wet.
   The hen will not.
2. I sped on my sled.
   I gave a yell to Nell.

Page 36

Review It! Word Families
-en, -et, -ell, -ed

Read the words in the box. Look at the picture.
Then write the correct word to finish the sentence.

| jet | pen | bell | red | sled |
| wet | ten | net | hen | well |

1. I have a red sled.
2. I hear a bell.
3. Ted is ten.
4. I get wet.
5. Where is the hen?

Look at the picture. Then write a sentence about it.

Answers will vary.

Page 37

Review It! Word Families
-en, -et, -ell, -ed

Look at the picture.
Then use the words in the box to write a sentence on the lines.

wet? hen get Will the

Will the hen get wet?

Nell my sled. sped on

Nell sped on my sled.

Use the words in the box, plus some of your own words, to write a sentence. Then draw a picture about it.

hen red

Answers will vary.

Spell It!
Skills: Reading and writing CVC and CCVC words, Understanding word meaning, Identifying spelling patterns

-ig	-in
big	pin
wig	win
dig	chin

Look at the picture. Write the correct word in the boxes.

1. w i g
2. p i n
3. d i g
4. c h i n
5. w i n
6. b i g

Circle the **-ig** words. Underline the **-in** words.

-ig	-in
fig pin big fin wig tin
twin jig grin chin dig twig

Write It!

Read the sentence. Trace the sentence.
Then write the sentence on the lines below.

1. Is this Miss Tig?
   Is this Miss Tig?
2. Is her fig big?
   Is her fig big?
3. Make fig jam.
   Make fig jam.
4. Win a pin.
   Win a pin.

Read It!
Skills: Reading simple sentences, Demonstrating comprehension

Read the sentence. Then draw a line to the correct picture.

1. I have a fin.
2. I have a grin.
3. I dig and dig.
4. I jig and jump.

Look at the picture. Then write the correct word to finish the sentence.

wig   swig   fig

1. Try a fig
2. Take a swig
3. Try on a wig

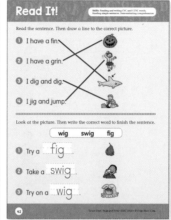

Find It!
Skills: Visual discrimination, Writing sentences with CVC and CCVC words

Find the words in the word search. Circle them.
Then write a ☑ in the box.

☑ wig   ☑ twig   ☑ dig   ☑ big
☑ twin ☑ fin   ☑ chin ☑ pin

```
w d o l t p f i n m i x m
i c l w z d i k u e c o
g c l a i e i g r c h i n
z d a p n m g z n r j u q
v c p v s t i l p b i g i
t w i g z j u m p i n l s
```

Now use four of the words you found to write a sentence.

Answers will vary.

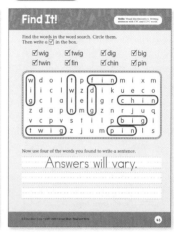

Spell It!
Skills: Reading and writing CVC and CCVC words, Understanding word meaning, Identifying spelling patterns

-ip	-it
rip	sit
chip	hit
lip	bit

Look at the picture. Write the correct word in the boxes.

1. r i p
2. c h i p
3. b i t
4. h i t
5. l i p
6. s i t

Circle the **-ip** words. Underline the **-it** words.

-ip	-it
kit tip sit sip whip fit
hip it lit zip quit drip

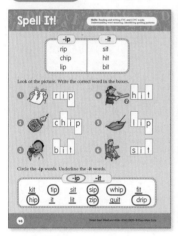

Write It!

Read the sentence. Trace the sentence.
Then write the sentence on the lines below.

1. He will clip it.
   He will clip it.
2. She will dip it.
   She will dip it.
3. Gabe can knit it.
   Gabe can knit it.
4. Will it fit?
   Will it fit?

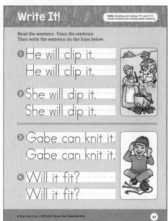

Read It!
Skills: Reading and writing CVC and CCVC words, Reading and writing simple sentences

Read the sentence. Then draw a line to the correct picture.

1. It likes to sit.
2. We like to knit.
3. He took a sip.
4. She took a chip.

Look at the picture. Then write the correct word to finish the sentence.

sit   trip   ship

1. Take a trip
2. Go on a ship
3. You can sit

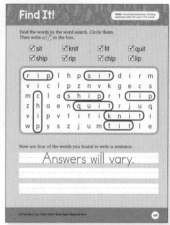

Find It!
Skills: Visual discrimination, Writing sentences with CVC and CCVC words

Find the words in the word search. Circle them.
Then write a ☑ in the box.

☑ sit   ☑ knit   ☑ fit   ☑ quit
☑ ship ☑ rip   ☑ chip ☑ lip

```
r i p l h p s i t d i r m
v i c l p z n v k g e c s
m c l a s h i p r t l i p
z h a e n q u i t r j u q
v i p v t i t i k n i t i
w p y s z j u m f i t l e
```

Now use four of the words you found to write a sentence.

Answers will vary.

Review It! *Word Families* -ig, -in, -ip, -it

Say the picture name. Listen for the ending sound.
Then draw a line to the correct word family.

-ig
-in
-ip
-it

Follow the directions shown below. Circle **-ig** words. Draw a box around **-in** words. Underline **-ip** words. Draw an X above **-it** words.

| -ig | -in | -ip | -it |

fig tin whip tip twig
hit twin sip quit fit
win jig big drip fin

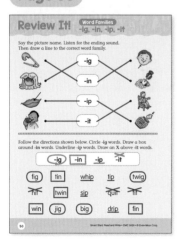

Review It! *Word Families* -ig, -in, -ip, -it

Say the picture name. Which word family do you hear?
Write **ig, in, ip,** or **it** to spell each word.

-ig -in -ip -it

1. wig
2. win
3. sip
4. sit
5. dip
6. dig
7. twig
8. twin

Read the sentences. Then draw a line to the correct picture.

1. This fig is thin.
   Did it win?
2. I took a chip.
   I bit it.

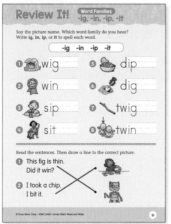

Review It! *Word Families* -ig, -in, -ip, -it

Read the words in the box. Look at the picture.
Then write the correct word to finish the sentence.

| fin | ship | dig | fig | win |
| knit | grin | chip | sip | twin |

1. Would you like a sip ?
2. This is how to knit
3. It has a fin
4. It is a little fig
5. It has a grin

Look at the picture. Then write a sentence about it.

Answers will vary.

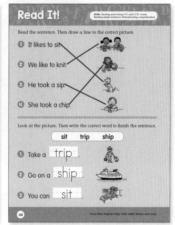

Review It! *Word Families* -ig, -in, -ip, -it

Look at the picture.
Then use the words in the box to write a sentence on the lines.

Miss win? Did Tig

Did Miss Tig win?

went on He a trip.

He went on a trip.

Use the words in the box, plus some of your own words, to write a sentence. Then draw a picture about it.

grin big

Answers will vary.

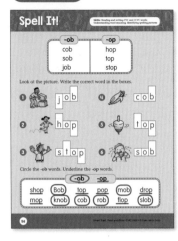

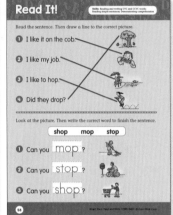

Page 56

Spell It!

-ob	-op
cob	hop
sob	top
job	stop

Look at the picture. Write the correct word in the boxes.

1. j o b
2. h o p
3. s t o p
4. c o b
5. t o p
6. s o b

Circle the -ob words. Underline the -op words.

(shop) (Bob) top pop (mob) drop
mop (knob) (cob) rob flop (slob)

Page 57

Write It!

Read the sentence. Trace the sentence. Then write the sentence on the lines below.

1. This is Bob's job.
   This is Bob's job.
2. He sells a knob.
   He sells a knob.
3. Visit Bob's shop.
   Visit Bob's shop.
4. Buy a mop.
   Buy a mop.

Page 58

Read It!

Read the sentence. Then draw a line to the correct picture.

1. I like it on the cob.
2. I like my job.
3. I like to hop.
4. Did they drop?

Look at the picture. Then write the correct word to finish the sentence.

shop   mop   stop

1. Can you mop ?
2. Can you stop ?
3. Can you shop ?

Page 59

Solve It!

Read the clue. What is the mystery word? Read the -ob and -op words below to find it. Write the mystery word next to the clue.

-ob		-op	
job	Bob	shop	drop
mob	sob	hop	mop

Clue	Mystery word
1. a bunny does this	hop
2. Mom will _____ for food.	shop
3. You use it to clean.	mop
4. a boy's name	Bob
5. You work at a _____	job
6. When you cry a lot you _____	sob

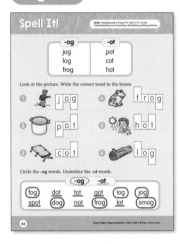

Page 62

Spell It!

-og	-ot
jog	pot
log	cot
frog	hot

Look at the picture. Write the correct word in the boxes.

1. j o g
2. p o t
3. c o t
4. f r o g
5. h o t
6. l o g

Circle the -og words. Underline the -ot words.

(fog) dot tot got (log) (jog)
spot (dog) not (frog) lot smog

Page 63

Write It!

Read the sentence. Trace the sentence. Then write the sentence on the lines below.

1. My dog is Dot.
   My dog is Dot.
2. Dot can trot.
   Dot can trot.
3. Frog is on a log.
   Frog is on a log.
4. Frog is off a log.
   Frog is off a log.

Page 64

Read It!

Read the sentence. Then draw a line to the correct picture.

1. I went for a jog.
2. I ran over a log.
3. Is it fog or smog?
4. Is it a dog or a frog?

Look at the picture. Then write the correct word to finish the sentence.

knot   clog   spot

1. It has a spot .
2. It has a knot .
3. It has a clog .

Page 65

Solve It!

Read the clue. What is the mystery word? Read the -og and -ot words below to find it. Write the mystery word next to the clue.

-og		-ot	
dog	log	spot	knot
frog	jog	tot	got

Clue	Mystery word
1. when you run	jog
2. a part of a tree	log
3. This is a pet.	dog
4. a small child	tot
5. a green animal	frog
6. This is hard to untie.	knot

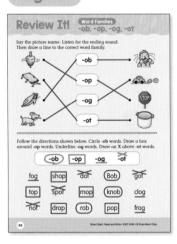
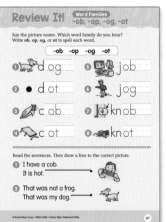

Page 66

Review It! Word Families -ob, -op, -og, -ot

Say the picture name. Listen for the ending sound. Then draw a line to the correct word family.

-ob
-op
-og
-ot

Follow the directions shown below. Circle -ob words. Draw a box around -op words. Underline -og words. Draw an X above -ot words.

-ob   -op   -og   -ot

fog   shop   dot   (Bob)   got
top   spot   mop   (knob)   clog
not   drop   (rob)   pop   frog

Page 67

Review It! Word Families -ob, -op, -og, -ot

Say the picture name. Which word family do you hear? Write ob, op, og, or ot to spell each word.

-ob   -op   -og   -ot

1. d og
2. d ot
3. c ob
4. c ot
5. j ob
6. j og
7. kn ob
8. kn ot

Read the sentences. Then draw a line to the correct picture.

1. I have a cob.
   It is hot.
2. That was not a frog.
   That was my dog.

Page 68

Review It! Word Families -ob, -op, -og, -ot

Read the words in the box. Look at the picture. Then write the correct word to finish the sentence.

| sob | cot | frog | tot | fog |
| shop | hot | top | log | hop |

1. Here is Bob's shop .
2. Sit on the log .
3. I am hot .
4. He is a little tot .
5. Why does he sob ?

Look at the picture. Then write a sentence about it.

Answers will vary.

Page 69

Review It! Word Families -ob, -op, -og, -ot

Look at the picture. Then use the words in the box to write a sentence on the lines.

is at shop. the Bob

Bob is at the shop.

The is on frog a log.

The frog is on a log.

Use the words in the box, plus some of your own words, to write a sentence. Then draw a picture about it.

spot   dog

Answers will vary.

Page 72
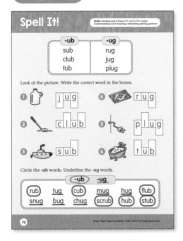

Page 73

Page 74

Page 75
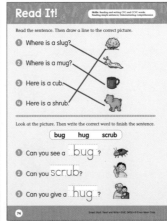

Page 78
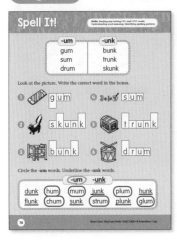

Page 79

Page 80
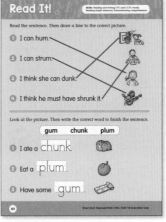

Page 81
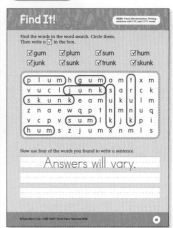

Page 82
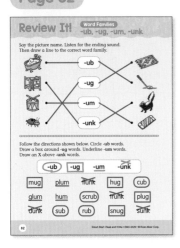

Page 83

Page 84

Page 85

Page 88

Spell It!
Skills: Reading and writing CVC and CCVC words. Understanding word meaning. Identifying spelling patterns

-ice	-ide
mice	hide
price	ride
slice	bride

Look at the picture. Write the correct word in the boxes.

1. hide
2. slice
3. ride
4. bride
5. price
6. mice

Circle the -ice words. Underline the -ide words.

(nice) wide (rice) (twice) side tide
slide (ice) (dice) glide (vice) hide

Page 89

Write It!
Skills: Reading and writing CVC and CCVC words. Reading and writing simple sentences.

Read the sentence. Trace the sentence.
Then write the sentence on the lines below.

1. We are nice mice.
We are nice mice.

2. We eat rice.
We eat rice.

3. I ride and ride.
I ride and ride.

4. I slide and glide.
I slide and glide.

Page 90

Read It!
Skills: Reading and writing CVC and CCVC words. Reading simple sentences. Demonstrating comprehension.

Read the sentence. Then draw a line to the correct picture.

1. Where did it hide?
2. Can you slide on it?
3. Do you want a slice?
4. Do you want the dice?

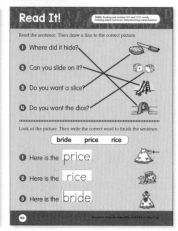

Look at the picture. Then write the correct word to finish the sentence.

bride   price   rice

1. Here is the price.
2. Here is the rice.
3. Here is the bride.

Page 91

Solve It!
Skills: Inference. Understanding word meaning. Writing CVC and CCVC words.

Read the clue. What is the mystery word? Read the -ice and -ide words below to find it. Write the mystery word next to the clue.

-ice		-ide	
slice	price	hide	slide
rice	mice	ride	tide

Clue	Mystery word
1. You _____ a bike.	ride
2. a _____ of bread	slice
3. how much you pay	price
4. small animals with tails	mice
5. You go down fast on this.	slide
6. These are small and white.	rice

Page 94

Spell It!
Skills: Reading and writing CVC and CCVC words. Understanding word meaning. Identifying spelling patterns.

-old	-ow
gold	bow
fold	mow
sold	crow

Look at the picture. Write the correct word in the boxes.

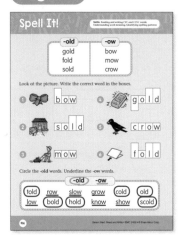

1. bow
2. sold
3. mow
4. gold
5. crow
6. fold

Circle the -old words. Underline the -ow words.

(told) row slow grow (cold) (old)
low (bold) (hold) know show (scold)

Page 95

Write It!
Skills: Reading and writing CVC and CCVC words. Reading and writing simple sentences.

Read the sentence. Trace the sentence.
Then write the sentence on the lines below.

1. This is cold.
This is cold.

2. It is cold to hold.
It is cold to hold.

3. Look at the snow.
Look at the snow.

4. Call for a tow.
Call for a tow.

Page 96

Read It!
Skills: Reading and writing CVC and CCVC words. Reading simple sentences. Demonstrating comprehension.

Read the sentence. Then draw a line to the correct picture.

1. Yours are old.
2. His is gold.
3. Hers is cold.
4. Min's has a bow.

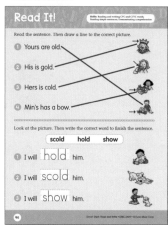

Look at the picture. Then write the correct word to finish the sentence.

scold   hold   show

1. I will hold him.
2. I will scold him.
3. I will show him.

Page 97

Solve It!
Skills: Inference. Understanding word meaning. Writing CVC and CCVC words.

Read the clue. What is the mystery word? Read the -old and -ow words below to find it. Write the mystery word next to the clue.

-old		-ow	
gold	sold	slow	know
hold	cold	grow	row

Clue	Mystery word
1. I am not warm, I am _____.	cold
2. _____ on!	hold
3. It is not fast, it is _____.	slow
4. This is a color.	gold
5. We _____ the car.	sold
6. Do you _____ him?	know

Page 100

Spell It!
Skills: Reading and writing CVC and CCVC words. Understanding word meaning. Identifying spelling patterns.

-ue	-une
glue	June
Sue	tune
clue	dune

Look at the picture. Write the correct word in the boxes.

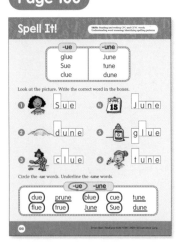

1. Sue
2. dune
3. clue
4. June
5. glue
6. tune

Circle the -ue words. Underline the -une words.

(due) prune (blue) (cue) tune
(flue) (true) June (Sue) dune

Page 101

Write It!
Skills: Reading and writing CVC and CCVC words. Reading and writing simple sentences.

Read the sentence. Trace the sentence.
Then write the sentence on the lines below.

1. I am happy in June.
I am happy in June.

2. I hum a tune.
I hum a tune.

3. Sue reads a book.
Sue reads a book.

4. The book is true.
The book is true.

Page 102

Read It!
Skills: Reading and writing CVC and CCVC words. Reading simple sentences. Demonstrating comprehension.

Read the sentence. Then draw a line to the correct picture.

1. I have some glue.
2. I have a prune.
3. The sky is blue.
4. The book is true.

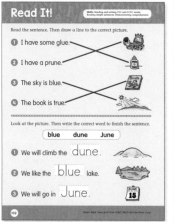

Look at the picture. Then write the correct word to finish the sentence.

blue   dune   June

1. We will climb the dune.
2. We like the blue lake.
3. We will go in June.

Page 103

Find It!
Skills: Visual discrimination. Writing sentences with CVC and CCVC words.

Find the words in the word search. Circle them.
Then write a ✓ in the box.

☑ blue   ☑ true   ☑ due   ☑ clue
☑ tune   ☑ june   ☑ dune   ☑ prune

```
r t o l b p s w a s i x m
v r c d l z n j u n e c d
m u r u u p r u n e w l u
z e a e q p z t k j u n e
v c p v s t u n e n a p e
c l u e z j u m x n t l s
```

Now use four of the words you found to write a sentence.

Answers will vary.

Page 106

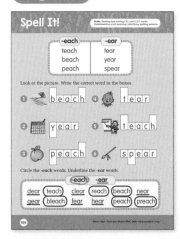

Spell It!

-each	-ear
teach	tear
beach	year
peach	spear

Look at the picture. Write the correct word in the boxes.

1. b e a c h
2. y e a r
3. p e a c h
4. t e a r
5. t e a c h
6. s p e a r

Circle the -each words. Underline the -ear words.

-each	-ear
dear (teach) clear (reach) (beach) near	gear (bleach) fear hear (peach) (preach)

Page 107

Write It!

Read the sentence. Trace the sentence.
Then write the sentence on the lines below.

1. The beach is near.
   The beach is near.
2. I can hear it.
   I can hear it.
3. Here is the beach.
   Here is the beach.
4. Dad will teach me.
   Dad will teach me.

Page 108

Read It!

Read the sentence. Then draw a line to the correct picture.

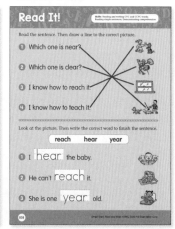

1. Which one is near?
2. Which one is clear?
3. I know how to reach it!
4. I know how to teach it!

Look at the picture. Then write the correct word to finish the sentence.

| reach | hear | year |

1. I hear the baby.
2. He can't reach it.
3. She is one year old.

Page 109

Find It!

Find the words in the word search. Circle them.
Then write a ☑ in the box.

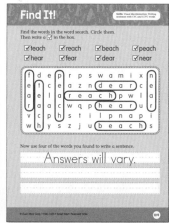

☑teach ☑reach ☑beach ☑peach
☑hear ☑fear ☑dear ☑near

f	d	e	p	r	p	s	w	a	m	i	x	n
t	e	i	c	e	a	z	n	d	e	a	r	c
a	r	a	c	l	a	r	e	a	c	h	p	w	l	a
v	c	a	c	w	q	p	h	e	a	r	u	r
w	p	h	s	t	i	l	p	n	a	p	i
h	y	s	z	j	u	b	e	a	c	h	s

Now use four of the words you found to write a sentence.

Answers will vary.

Page 112

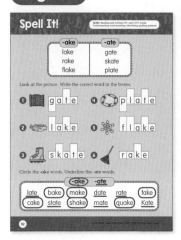

Spell It!

-ake	-ate
lake	gate
rake	skate
flake	plate

Look at the picture. Write the correct word in the boxes.

1. g a t e
2. l a k e
3. s k a t e
4. p l a t e
5. f l a k e
6. r a k e

Circle the -ake words. Underline the -ate words.

-ake	-ate
late (bake) (make) date rate fake	cake state (shake) mate (quake) Kate

Page 113

Write It!

Read the sentence. Trace the sentence.
Then write the sentence on the lines below.

1. Bake a cake.
   Bake a cake.
2. It is for Jake.
   It is for Jake.
3. There is Kate.
   There is Kate.
4. She can skate.
   She can skate.

Page 114

Read It!

Read the sentence. Then draw a line to the correct picture.

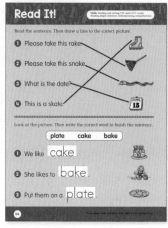

1. Please take this rake.
2. Please take this snake.
3. What is the date?
4. This is a skate.

Look at the picture. Then write the correct word to finish the sentence.

| plate | cake | bake |

1. We like cake.
2. She likes to bake.
3. Put them on a plate.

Page 115

Solve It!

Read the clue. What is the mystery word? Read the -ake and -ate words below to find it. Write the mystery word next to the clue.

-ake	-ate
flake bake late skate	shake lake gate state

Clue	Mystery word
1. a large body of water	lake
2. Dad will _____ a cake.	bake
3. not on time	late
4. a shoe with wheels	skate
5. Close the _____.	gate
6. to move up and down	shake

Page 116

Review It! Word Families
-ice, -ide, -old, -ow

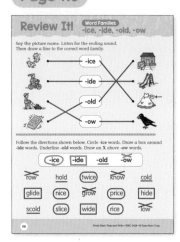

Say the picture name. Listen for the ending sound.
Then draw a line to the correct word family.

- -ice
- -ide
- -old
- -ow

Follow the directions shown below. Circle -ice words. Draw a box around -ide words. Underline -old words. Draw an X above -ow words.

| -ice | -ide | -old | -ow |

row hold twice know cold
glide nice grow price hide
scold slice wide rice low

Page 117

Review It! Word Families
-ue, -une, -each, -ear

Say the picture name. Which word family do you hear?
Write ue, une, each, or ear to spell each word.

| -ue | -une | -each | -ear |

1. t ear
2. p each
3. June J une
4. t une
5. sp ear
6. t each
7. gl ue
8. cl ue

Read the sentences. Then draw a line to the correct picture.

1. I am happy in June.
   I hum a tune.
2. The beach is near.
   I can hear it.

Page 118

Review It! Word Families
-ake, -ate

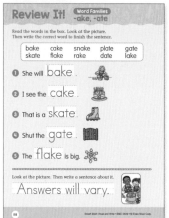

Read the words in the box. Look at the picture.
Then write the correct word to finish the sentence.

| bake | cake | snake | plate | gate |
| skate | flake | rake | date | lake |

1. She will bake.
2. I see the cake.
3. That is a skate.
4. Shut the gate.
5. The flake is big.

Look at the picture. Then write a sentence about it.

Answers will vary.

Page 119

Review It! Word Families
-ice, -each, -ue, -ate

Look at the picture.
Then use the words in the box to write a sentence on the lines.

a beach. There is at clue the

There is a clue
at the beach.

is plate. rice This on a

This rice is on
a plate.

Use the words in the box, plus some of your own words, to write a sentence. Then draw a picture about it.

gate blue

Answers will vary.

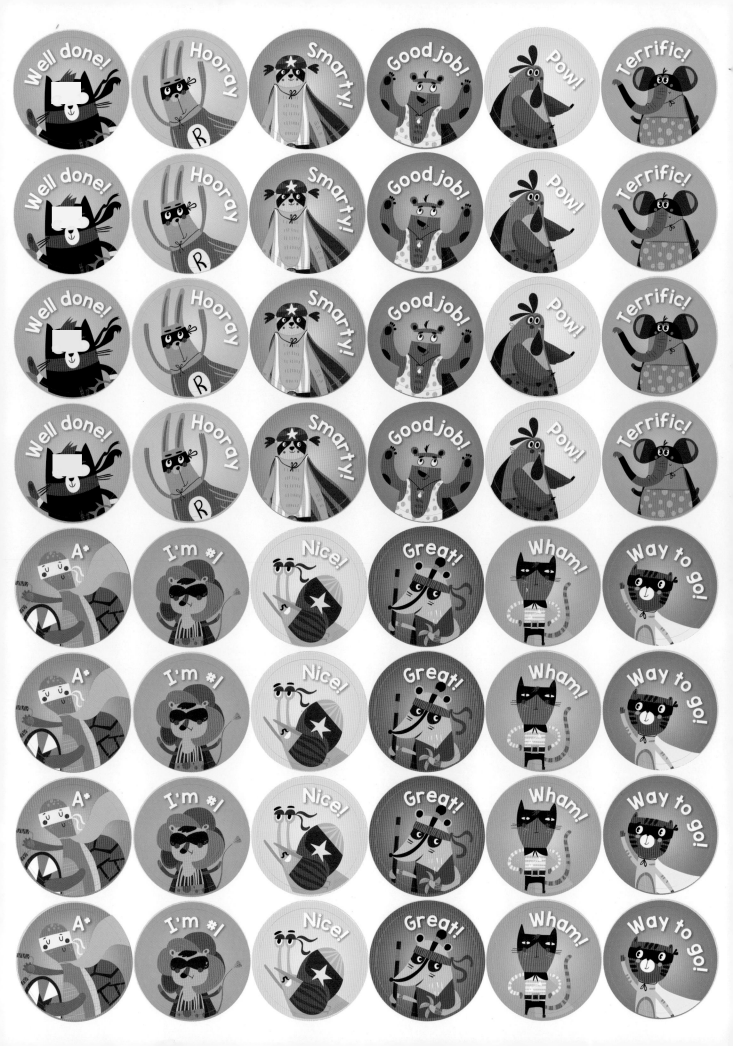